My Big Book of 5-Minute Devotions

My
Big Book of
5-Minute
Devotions

CELEBRATING GOD'S WORLD

Written by Pamela Kennedy with Douglas Kennedy
Illustrated by Amy Wummer

WORTHY®
kids

ISBN: 978-0-8249-5556-4

WorthyKids
Hachette Book Group
1290 Avenue of the Americas
New York, NY 10104

Color separations by Precision Color Graphics, Franklin, Wisconsin

Printed and bound in Canada
FRI
15 14 13

Designed by Georgina Chidlow-Irvin

Scripture quotations are taken from the *Holy Bible*, New Living
Translation, copyright © 1996. Used by permission of Tyndale
House Publishers, Inc., Wheaton, Illinois 60189. All rights reserved.

Library of Congress Cataloging-in-Publication Data

Kennedy, Pamela, date.
  My big book of 5-minute devotions : celebrating
God's world / written by Pamela Kennedy with
Douglas Kennedy ; illustrated by Amy Wummer.
    p. cm.
  Includes index.
  ISBN-13: 978-0-8249-5556-4 (alk. paper)
  ISBN-10: 0-8249-5556-0 (alk. paper)
 1. Animals—Religious aspects—Christianity—Juvenile
literature. I. Kennedy, Douglas, date. II. Wummer,
Amy. III. Title. IV. Title: My big book of five-minute
devotions.
  BT746.K45 2007
  242'.62—dc22
                        2006101443

Contents

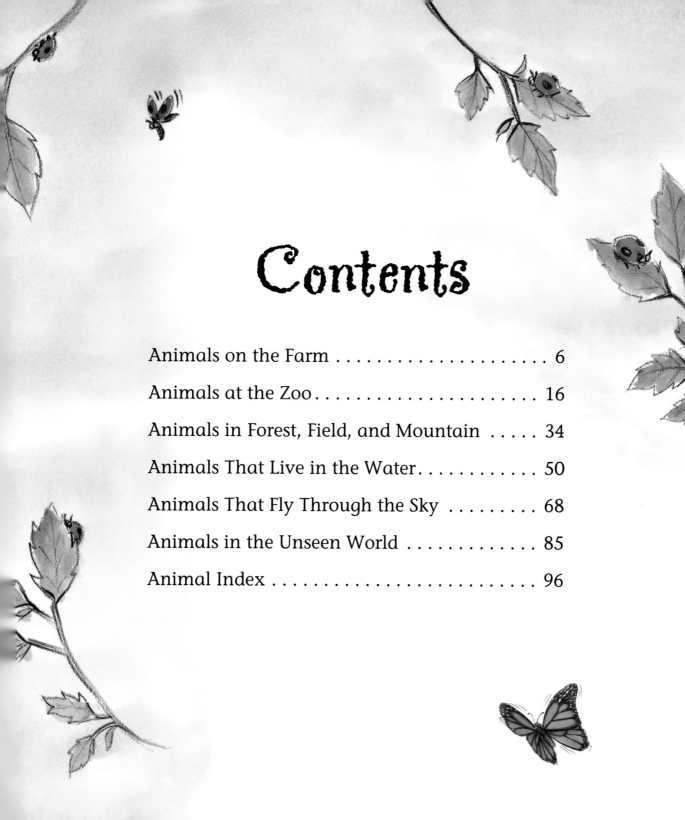

Animals on the Farm

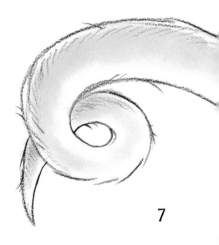

Farmers take care of many different kinds of animals. Some of the animals help the farmers too. The Bible tells us that God created both people and animals and said that they were good. When we care for animals, we are showing that we believe what God said.

All God's creatures share the earth and each has a very special place. On the farm we meet animals that live around people. Some farm animals do work and others just like to play. Farmers enjoy helping their animals and make sure that the animals are healthy and happy. If you have a pet or farm animal, you have a special responsibility to take good care of it too.

Dogs on the Job

Dogs enjoy playing and running, digging in the snow, or catching a Frisbee on a summer afternoon. But did you know that some dogs also have jobs? There are dogs that have been trained to help people who cannot see. They keep their owners safe by guiding them around dangerous objects or helping them cross a busy street. Other dogs help people who cannot hear. They let their owners know when the phone is ringing or when a baby is crying and needs help. Some dogs work in airports to sniff for things that should not be taken on planes. Other dogs hunt for people who are lost in the snow or in dark places where people cannot see. When these dogs are working, they know it is important to stay on the job. When they are finished working, then it's time to play.

Just like dogs, children love to run and play too. But God tells us that we also have work or chores we need to do. Some children help their parents by cleaning up after meal times. Other children help take care of their younger brothers and sisters. Taking out the trash, folding clothes, and picking up toys are other chores children can do. In every family there is work that needs to be done. God wants us to work hard and to do our jobs without complaining. When the work is done, then everyone has time to play!

What do you say?

- Are the dogs in the picture working or playing?

- What kinds of work can dogs do?

- What are some chores you do at your home?

- Why do you think God wants us to do our work without complaining?

What does God say?

Commit your work to the LORD, and then your plans will succeed.
PROVERBS 16:3

Smart Pigs

Lots of people think pigs are messy, smelly, lazy, and stupid. But people who really know pigs, like farmers and veterinarians, can tell us a different story. They know that pigs like being clean and that clean pigs don't stink. Pigs are also very active animals, and some people even train their pigs to run at special pig racetracks. But the most surprising thing about pigs is how smart they are. Animal experts agree that pigs are some of the smartest animals in the world. They learn quickly, and they can be trained to do all kinds of things. That's why so many people think pigs make wonderful house pets!

Even though pigs are clean, smart, and friendly, people tell stories that make pigs seem lazy and stupid. It isn't fair to pigs when people say mean things about them—especially because those things aren't true. Sometimes people like to judge others and say mean things about them, even when it's not true. God doesn't want us to waste our time judging others, and he doesn't like it when we say mean things that aren't true. He wants us to accept each other and be kind.

What do you say?

- What kinds of things are these pigs doing?

- What are some untrue things people have said about pigs?

- Have you ever said untrue things about someone else?

- Why doesn't God want us to judge others?

What does God say?

Stop judging others, and you will not be judged. Stop criticizing others, or it will all come back on you. If you forgive others, you will be forgiven.

LUKE 6:37

11

Wild Horses

In jumping contests, trained horses leap over fences. In rodeos, horses help cowboys rope calves. All these horses began as babies, or foals, that had to be trained. Horses do not naturally allow people to ride on their backs. But when horses have been trained, they can accomplish many different things like pulling carts, running in races, or working on ranches. Without training, a horse may be wild and beautiful, but it cannot help anyone.

Just like horses, we all need to learn to do certain things. We do not naturally know how to be polite, to say "please" and "thank you," to pick up after ourselves, or to help others. Our parents and teachers must train us to do these things or we cannot be helpful to ourselves or to others. God knows that it is important for each of us to learn and grow. He knows we need people to help train us. But we need to be willing to learn and grow too. When we are willing to follow the directions our parents and teachers give us, we become better helpers.

What do you say?

- Can you find the foal in the picture?

- What are some things your parents are teaching you to do?

- Why do horses need to be trained?

- Why do you think God wants you to obey your parents and teachers?

What does God say?

Children, obey your parents because you belong to the Lord, for this is the right thing to do.
EPHESIANS 6:1

13

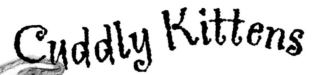

Cuddly Kittens

When kittens are born, they are very small. Their little eyes aren't even open until a week or two later. They cannot walk well and they need their mothers to take very good care of them so they will be safe. They can be hurt easily if they are not held carefully, or if they are squeezed too tightly. Kittens need to stay warm too. If they get too cold, they could die. But if a kitten is well cared for by its mother, and if it is protected while it is still very young, it will grow up to be a healthy, happy cat.

It is good to be gentle and to protect baby animals from harm, to treat them with kindness and to care for them. But sometimes people need special care too. There are times when we all feel weak or small. We might be frightened or just not very strong in some way. That's when we need family and friends to help and protect us. God knows that we are all weak at times and he wants us to show gentleness and love to one another. He wants us to help and care for each other so we can all grow up to be healthy and happy people.

What do you say?

- What are these kittens doing?

- Why do you think God wants you to be a kind and gentle friend?

- When have you felt like you needed someone to protect and care for you?

- Why do kittens need to be protected?

What does God say?

Gentle words bring life and health.
PROVERBS 15:4A

15

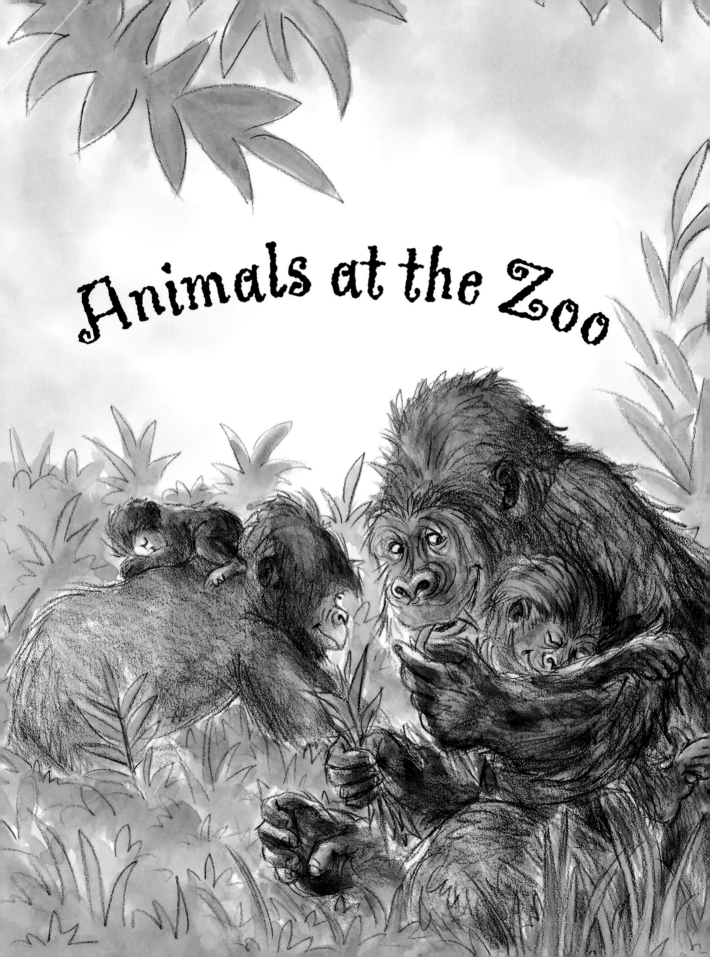

Animals at the Zoo

There are hundreds of different kinds of animals that live all over the world. Some of them are disappearing because they cannot find food or water. People who want to help these animals survive have created zoos. In zoos animals are safe because zookeepers protect them and learn how to help them live longer and healthier lives.

When we go to the zoo, we can see the wonderful variety of animals that God created and find out about how we can help them too. When we learn how to protect wild animals, we are showing our love for God by protecting what he has made.

Three-Toed Patience

Three-toed sloths live in the rain forest and spend their entire lives climbing around in trees. They take their time, patiently searching for just the right leaves to eat. In fact, sloths move so slowly that tiny plants called algae grow in their fur. After a long time, the algae turns their fur coats green. Slow-moving sloths use their green coats to blend in with the trees and hide from their enemies. It's hard for hunters like jaguars and eagles to find a little, green sloth in a big, green forest. Because sloths are slow and patient, they become almost invisible in the trees, safe from all the dangers around.

It is not always easy to be patient. Sometimes we do not want to wait for things. We want them right now. But getting things right now may not be best for us. Being patient with God means waiting for him to show us the best time for things. Sometimes it can be very hard to wait, but God promises us that if we are patient, he will help us grow in ways that are safe. God knows just the right time for everything.

What do you say?

- Can you find the sloths hiding in the trees?

- What makes the sloth's fur coat turn green?

- When did you have to be patient?

- Why is it important for you to be patient with God?

What does God say?

I waited patiently for the LORD to help me, and he turned to me and heard my cry.

PSALM 40:1

19

Safety Stripes

Zebras look like horses with beautiful black and white stripes. Their stripes are pretty, but they are also important for the zebras' safety. When zebras are traveling across the open plains of Africa, it can be very dangerous. Lions wait to pounce on one that is slow or sick. So sometimes hundreds of zebras come together to travel in one giant herd! When lots of zebras get close to each other, all their stripes seem to blend together. This confuses the lions. It is hard for them to pick out one zebra to chase. The zebras know that if they stick together, they will all be safe from the lions.

We can learn a lesson from these beautiful, striped animals. There are times when it is difficult for us to be all by ourselves too. God knows that we are happier and safer when we learn to work together. This is called teamwork, or cooperation. When we cooperate with one another, we can have lots of fun. We can play games, act out stories, solve problems, and even help each other. The hard things seem easier when we can share them with others. It pleases God to see us work together. Because he made us, he knows we do our best when we learn to use teamwork.

What do you say?

- Can you count all the zebras in the picture?

- What happens when hundreds of zebras work together?

- What are some things you like to do with your friends?

- Why is teamwork important to God?

What does God say?

Then make me truly happy by agreeing wholeheartedly with each other, loving one another, and working together with one heart and purpose.

PHILIPPIANS 2:2

21

Strange Friends

In the grasslands of southern Africa are two strange friends. One is the redbilled oxpecker, a brown and yellow bird with a bright red bill. Its best friend is the rhinoceros! If you look closely at rhinos you will often see oxpeckers riding along on their backs or climbing on their heads. The rhino likes to give the little bird a ride, because the oxpecker keeps the huge animal healthy and clean by eating pesky flies, ticks, fleas, and dead skin. Another way the bird helps the rhino is by making a sharp call when it sees danger. This helps the rhino because he doesn't see very well. The oxpecker and the rhino may seem like strange friends, but they help one another every day.

Just like the bird and the rhino, people need friends too. God knows that we would be lonely without friends. Friends help one another in many ways. We listen to each other, play together, work together, and share what we have. The Bible teaches us to treat our friends the way we would like to be treated.

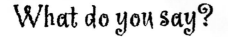

What do you say?

• Can you find all the oxpeckers in the picture?

• How do the oxpecker and the rhino help each other?

• What are some of the things you do to help your friends?

• Why do you think God wants us to be good friends to each other?

What does God say?

Do for others what you would like them to do for you.
MATTHEW 7:12A

Talented Aardvarks

The aardvark is an odd-looking animal that spends its days sleeping and its nights hunting for its favorite food—ants! This shy animal is especially suited for hunting these insects. It has large ears, able to listen for danger, and a sensitive nose that can sniff out any signs of an anthill. The aardvark runs along close to the ground on short legs, and when it finds an insect nest, the hungry aardvark quickly digs into it with powerful front feet and strong claws. When the nest is opened, the aardvark sticks its snout into the hole and searches for ants with its long, sticky tongue. The aardvark can close its nostrils so insects can't run up its nose, and its thick skin protects it from the bites of the angry ants. Even though the aardvark is a timid animal, it has everything it needs to be a great ant hunter.

Just like the aardvark, you have been given special gifts and abilities by God too. Perhaps you can run fast or read well. Maybe you can do math problems with ease or sing and dance. You might be especially good at making others happy or doing kind things. God knows each one of his children, and he has given each of us exactly what we need to succeed.

What do you say?

• What is the aardvark doing in the picture?

• What are some things you can do well?

• What are some of the things that make the aardvark such a good ant hunter?

• Why do you think God gives each of us special talents and abilities?

What does God say?

God has given each of us the ability to do certain things well. ROMANS 12:6A

Angry Hippos

If you looked at a hippopotamus yawning in a slow-moving African river, you might think it is a friendly and lazy animal. But you would be mistaken! Armed with long, razor-sharp teeth, the hippo is actually one of the most dangerous African animals. What makes it so dangerous is its temper. If a boat comes too close, the hippopotamus will lunge out with a loud roar and slash at it. The boat may be overturned and any riders bitten or dragged under water and drowned. When hippos fight with one another, they may battle for an hour or more, leaving each other gashed and bleeding! These animals may look peaceful, but don't make them mad!

Sometimes people can have nasty tempers just like the hippo. They are just fine until someone bothers them. Then they use angry words or even fists to fight. They hurt other people and lose friends. No one likes to be around someone who gets mad and always wants to fight. God tells us to be friends and to settle our differences peacefully. He knows that when we lose our tempers, we hurt others and ourselves too.

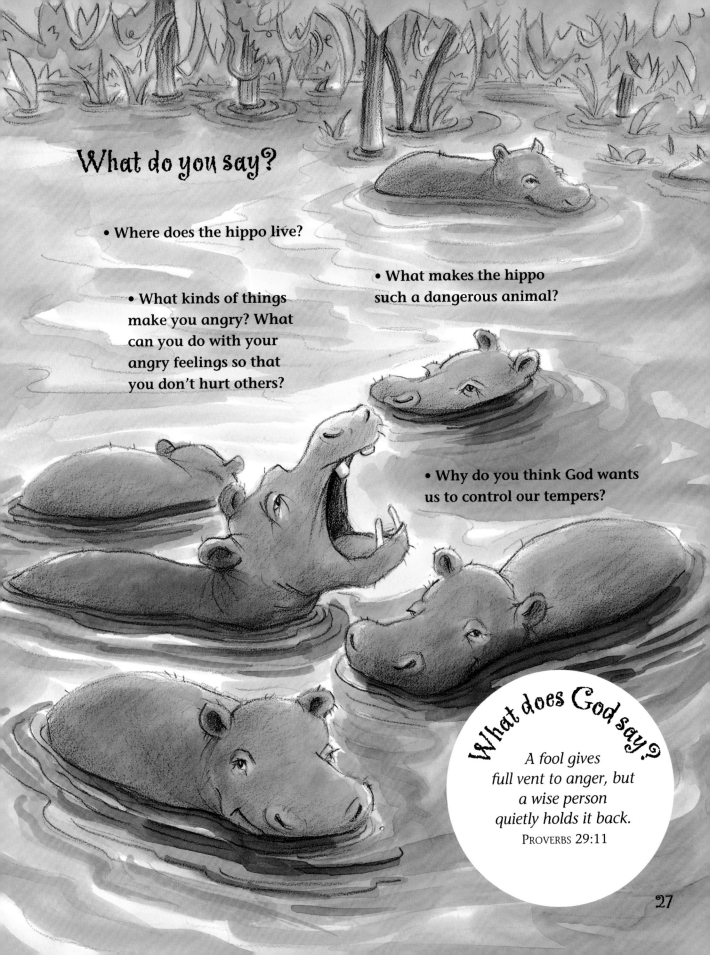

What do you say?

- Where does the hippo live?

- What kinds of things make you angry? What can you do with your angry feelings so that you don't hurt others?

- What makes the hippo such a dangerous animal?

- Why do you think God wants us to control our tempers?

What does God say?

A fool gives full vent to anger, but a wise person quietly holds it back.

PROVERBS 29:11

Masked Meerkats

The markings on meerkats make them look like bandits. They look like little thieves because they have black stripes across their faces that look like masks. However, meerkats are not selfish like thieves; in fact, they're very friendly and helpful. Meerkats live in groups, called bands, with as many as forty members. Everyone in the band helps everyone else stay safe and get food. When a mother meerkat needs to go out and get food, other meerkats take turns babysitting the youngsters, even if it means missing lunch. When all the meerkats are out searching for food, one meerkat will climb a nearby tree to watch for danger. If it sees a hawk or a snake, it will call out to its friends below so they can run for safety. Meerkats also take care of each other by cleaning one another's fur. Meerkats are great helpers. They love to make sure everybody in the whole band is healthy and happy.

God likes to see meerkats being such wonderful helpers. Imagine how hard it would be for a mother meerkat to feed herself and her babies if all the other meerkats were selfish and she couldn't get a babysitter! God gives us lots of chances to be helpers, too. It pleases him when we aren't selfish and help the people around us.

What do you say?

- Which meerkats are helping others?

- How do meerkats help the others in their band?

- What is the difference between being selfish and being a helper?

- Why do you think God wants you to be a helper?

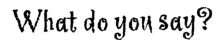

What does God say?

Don't be selfish. . . . Be humble, thinking of others as better than yourself.

PHILIPPIANS 2:3

29

Gorilla Families

Gorillas are the largest members of the ape family. They live in the mountains and lowlands of Africa. Although there are movies and stories about fierce, giant gorillas, most gorillas live quiet and peaceful lives in small family groups. Both father and mother gorillas help care for their children. They are patient teachers and spend many hours playing games with their babies. When little gorillas are tired or frightened, their parents will pick them up and hug them or carry them on their backs. Mother gorillas teach their children how to build sleeping nests and how to find good things to eat. Young gorillas enjoy climbing and wrestling just like human children.

God has placed people in families too. People in families protect and love one another. Just like the gorillas, we can learn many things in our families. We learn to work and play together, to respect one another, and to do our part to help the family. God says that he is like a father to all his children. In a very special way, everyone who loves God belongs to his family; and it pleases God when we love all our brothers and sisters.

What do you say?

- How many baby gorillas can you find in the picture?

- How many people are in your family? Can you name them all?

- What kinds of things do gorillas do in their families?

- Why do you think God places people in families?

What does God say?

Whenever we have the opportunity, we should do good to everyone, especially to our Christian brothers and sisters.
GALATIANS 6:10

31

Monkey Business

Spider monkeys live in the rain forests of Central and South America. They are some of the most acrobatic monkeys in the world. With their long arms and legs and their gripping tails, they can swing through the trees with speed and jump from branch to branch without falling. But when spider monkeys are young, they are not very graceful at all. They have to learn how to swing through the trees. Sometimes their mothers help them; but at other times, the young monkeys practice swinging from branch to branch by themselves. Sometimes they slip and fall. Then they must climb back up and try again. It takes lots of practice before they can travel through the trees as well as their parents.

Have you ever tried to do something that your older brother or sister or your parents can do? At first did it seem hard? When we are learning to do new things, we all make mistakes. Just like the spider monkey, we have to try over and over again until we get it right. Practice is a good way to get better at doing things. When you practice riding a bike, singing a song, spelling a word, or reading a book, you get better each time. Don't be afraid to practice—it's the only way to improve!

What do you say?

- How many spider monkeys do you see in the picture?

- What is something you have to practice?

- Why do the spider monkeys have to practice?

- Why do you think God wants us to keep learning new things?

What does God say?

Teach the wise and they will be wiser. Teach the righteous, and they will learn more.
PROVERBS 9:9

33

Animals in Forest, Field, and Mountain

Have you ever taken a walk in a forest, played in a field, or hiked up a mountain? If so, you might have seen some of the animals that live there. God has provided homes for animals in all kinds of places and each animal has a special way of taking care of itself and its family.

When we visit the places where animals live, we should not tease or disturb these creatures. If we are still and quiet, they will sometimes let us watch them, but if they are frightened, they might run away or try to hurt us. They are not being mean, they are just protecting themselves and their babies. Respecting animals is a way of showing our respect for God's creation.

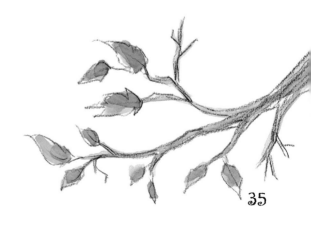

Fleecy Fighters

Sometimes animals just can't get along. Bighorn sheep live high in the mountains and are not very friendly at all. Male bighorn sheep are called rams, and every autumn they get angry and fight. They run toward each other and slam their heads together. None of them wants to share territory with any of the other rams, so they fight to see which ones are the strongest. The strongest rams with the biggest horns can stay, but the weak rams with small horns have to find someplace new to live. A fight between two rams can last an entire day, and sometimes the fight only ends when the stronger ram kills the weaker one!

Some people like to fight, just like rams. Sometimes, people who are big and strong think they can get what they want by hurting smaller people. It is hard to be friends with someone like that. People who use words to settle their problems make much better friends than people who use their size. God would rather see us talk about our problems. When we are peaceful and friendly, we understand each other better—and we understand God better too!

What do you say?

- Which ram has the biggest horns?

- What makes you want to act like an angry ram?

- Why do rams slam their heads together?

- Why does God want us to talk about our problems instead of fighting?

What does God say?

Stop your anger!
Turn from your rage!
Do not envy others—it
only leads to harm.
PSALM 37:8

37

Blind as Bats!

Many people say that a person who cannot find something is "as blind as a bat." Bats, however, have perfectly good eyes and can see fine in the daytime. But during the day, bats usually sleep hanging upside down by their feet. When night comes, bats leave their nesting areas or roosts and fly in search of their favorite food, juicy insects. Because it is dark at night, bats cannot use their eyes to find flying insects so they use their ears instead. Bats make rapid, high-pitched squeaks. These squeaks echo off insects and bounce back to the bat's very sensitive ears. By listening very carefully, the bat knows just where the insect is and can either catch it in its mouth or scoop it up with one of its webbed wings. By using its ears, the bat can find all it needs to survive.

People have ears that are not as sensitive as a bat's, but we need to listen too. God has given us ears to hear many things. We listen to words that teach us and warn us of danger. We hear beautiful music and funny stories. Our ears help us learn about God and his plans for us. Listening carefully is an important way to learn and grow.

What do you say?

• Look at the picture. Which bat is about to catch its dinner?

• What are some of your favorite sounds?

• How do bats "see" with their ears?

• Why do you think God wants his children to be good listeners?

What does God say?

My dear brothers and sisters, be quick to listen, slow to speak, and slow to get angry.
JAMES 1:19

Prickly Porcupines

The porcupine lives in the woods of North America. Some people have given this animal the nickname "pricklepig" because of its prickly spines. The porcupine has about three hundred thousand sharp quills covering its back, sides, and tail. When another animal comes too close, the porcupine makes its quills stand up. It looks like a giant pincushion! As soon as the curious animal tries to sniff or bite the porcupine, it gets a nose or mouthful of pain. Other animals soon learn to leave the prickly porcupine alone.

Have you ever known people who are like prickly porcupines? Whenever someone new comes along, they act unfriendly and pretty soon the new friend goes away. If we want to have friends, we need to be kind to people and talk with them. We can ask them questions, share our toys, and invite them to play with us. It pleases God when we are kind to others. When we are friendly to people, they will want to be friends with us. It's no fun being a lonely, prickly porcupine!

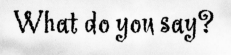

What do you say?

• What animal may get an unhappy surprise from the porcupine?

• Why does the porcupine have the nickname "pricklepig?"

• What can you do to be a friend to someone new?

• Why do you think God asks us to be kind to others?

What does God say?

Your own soul is nourished when you are kind, but you destroy yourself when you are cruel.

PROVERBS 11:17

41

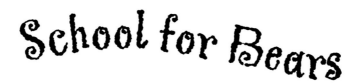

School for Bears

Grizzly bears are known for being large and very ferocious. They can be up to seven feet tall and weigh over five hundred pounds. But when grizzly cubs are born, they are very small and helpless. A newborn cub is blind and has no teeth and no fur. It is only eight inches long and weighs just over a pound. It's about the size of a big banana! But cubs grow fast. By the time the grizzly cub is a few months old, its mother is already teaching it many things. She shows her cubs how to find berries, roots, and nuts. She also teaches the cubs how to catch fish. Grizzlies like to stand beside a stream and scoop salmon out of the water with their big paws. The little cubs must practice many times before they catch their first fish. The mother teaches them to hunt, fish, and protect themselves from danger. They learn new things every day.

Just like bear cubs, people need to learn many things too. Our parents and teachers help us learn to read, to ride a bike, to tie our shoes, to dance, to play a musical instrument, and to understand about God and the Bible. Learning is fun and exciting and helps everyone grow.

What do you say?

- What do you think the cubs in the picture are learning?

- What do grizzly cubs look like when they are born?

- Name something you are learning to do.

- Why do you think God wants people to learn about him?

What does God say?

[Jesus said] . . .
Let me teach you,
because I am humble
and gentle, and you will
find rest for your souls.
MATTHEW 11:29

43

Watch Out for Wildcats!

Wildcats look very much like pet cats called tabbies. Their coats are marked with brown and tan stripes, and they have golden or green eyes. They look friendly; but if you ever meet one, look out! Wildcats are very dangerous and powerful. They become fierce fighters if they think another animal or a person is trespassing on their territory. They snarl, flatten their ears, arch their backs, and curl back their lips to show their long, sharp teeth. They will attack, scratching and biting, if they feel threatened or afraid. When a wildcat is angry, it is a good thing to stay far away!

Some people are like wildcats. They seem to be friendly; but when they become angry, they say and do things that are hurtful. God wants his children to be kind to one another and to control their anger. When we are angry we need to talk about how we feel instead of punching or hitting other people or calling them names. We can even tell God about being angry and ask him to help us control ourselves. Everyone gets angry sometimes, but no one should act like a wildcat!

What do you say?

• How can you tell that the wildcat in the picture is angry?

• What makes you angry? How do you act when you are angry?

• Why are wildcats dangerous?

• Why do you think God wants us to control ourselves when we are angry?

What does God say?

And don't sin by letting anger gain control over you. Don't let the sun go down while you are still angry, for anger gives a mighty foothold to the Devil.
EPHESIANS 4:26-27

45

Busy Beavers

The beaver is an animal that works very hard. Beavers build their homes, or dams, in streams and ponds. When a beaver wants to build a dam, it waddles on its short legs to find a small tree. Then the beaver begins gnawing at the tree trunk with its long, sharp front teeth. In just a few minutes, a busy beaver can cut down a trunk that is five inches thick. Then the beaver trims off the small branches, cuts the trunk in shorter lengths, and drags the heavy limbs back to the building site. Carefully, the beaver weaves sticks, branches, reeds, and small tree trunks together, then fills in the spaces with mud to make its dam secure. Even a good dam gets damaged, so the beaver must constantly be on the watch to repair holes caused by weather or other animals. Beavers never quit working. If they did, their homes might break apart and float away!

Just like the busy beaver, we sometimes have jobs that take time to finish. If we quit when we get tired or bored, the job will not get done. The Bible calls working hard and not giving up, *endurance*. If we have endurance, we will finish what we begin. We can be proud about doing good work, just like the busy beaver!

What do you say?

- Look at the picture. How many trees have these busy beavers cut down?

- How does a beaver build a new dam?

- What kind of work is hard for you to finish?

- Why do you think God wants us to have endurance?

What does God say?

. . . for when your endurance is fully developed, you will be strong in character and ready for anything.

James 1:4

47

Rattlesnake Warnings

The rattlesnake is a large desert reptile with a bad reputation. Usually the snake stays away from people; but if someone comes near the rattler, it will hold its tail upright and shake the end. There are several hollow rattles on the end of the snake's tail made of material just like your fingernails. When the snake shakes these, they make a buzzing sound that means, "Danger! Stay away!" If the rattler's warning is ignored, the snake will strike out and bite with poisonous fangs. The poison can make a person very sick. Some people even die from rattlesnake bites. If you ever hear a rattlesnake's warning, be sure to get away fast!

God doesn't want us to be hurt because we do not know about danger. That is why he gives us many warnings in the Bible. Just like the rattle of the rattlesnake, God's warnings tell us to stay away from things that are harmful. He tells us to stay away from lying, from stealing, from being selfish, and from being mean to others. If we follow God's warnings, we will be happier and safer. God warns us of these dangers because he loves us.

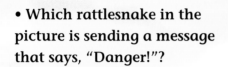

What do you say?

• Which rattlesnake in the picture is sending a message that says, "Danger!"?

• How can you know if a rattlesnake is getting ready to bite?

• What are some dangerous things you have been warned about?

• Why do you think God wants us to follow his warnings?

What does God say?

A prudent person foresees the danger ahead and takes precautions; the simpleton goes blindly on and suffers the consequences.

PROVERBS 22:3

49

Animals That Live in the Water

When you see a stream, a pond, or the ocean you may only notice the surface of the water, but under the water there is another world where many wonderful creatures live and play. We cannot live there because we must have air to breathe. But God has created many kinds of animals and fish that spend their lives in the water. They have special abilities to swim, dive, and play below the water's surface.

There are many different ways that some animals breathe, live, and move. Every animal was specially designed by God and its body is just right for that creature. God is so wise that he knows exactly what is best for each of us.

51

Strange Creatures

A platypus is a very unusual critter. The only place on the planet where we can find this weird animal is in the creeks and swamps of eastern Australia.

Platypuses have a bill like a duck but no feathers. Instead, they have fur like a cat. They have webbed feet like a seagull and a flat tail like a beaver. When they're upset, they can growl like a dog or strike out with their poison-tipped spurs. A platypus doesn't give birth like other furry animals—it lays eggs! It's safe to say that there is no other animal on earth like a platypus. In fact, when an explorer brought the first platypus to England, the people laughed at it. They said it wasn't even a real animal!

Sometimes we laugh at people who don't look like us. We make fun of them if they do things in ways that seem strange to us. This hurts their feelings and makes God sad too. God says he is the Father of all people. He has made each person. He knows where we will live and what we will look like. We should never try to make someone feel bad just because they don't look or act like us. God enjoys variety, and every person is a part of God's wonderful creation. He loves each of us equally.

What do you say?

- What is the platypus doing?

- What are some things that seem strange about the platypus?

- Has anyone ever hurt your feelings?

- Why do you think God wants us to try to understand others?

What does God say?

And yet, LORD, you are our Father. . . . We are all formed by your hand.
ISAIAH 64:8

53

Playful Sea Otters

The sea otter spends almost all of its life in the water. Otters love to dive and splash and swim from morning to night. The otter's favorite foods are abalone and sea urchins. These both have hard shells, but the clever little otter has figured out a way to crack them open. The otter finds a stone or smooth rock, tucks it under its front leg, scoops up an abalone or urchin, and then back-floats on the surface of the water with the stone resting on its tummy. Grabbing the shellfish, the otter smacks it against the stone until it cracks. Then he eats the juicy meat inside the shell. After all this hard work, the otter is tired. He makes his bed in the water too. The otter rolls up in a long piece of seaweed then falls asleep, cozy in the kelp blanket while the soft waves rock him to sleep.

Just like sea otters, children love to play all day. After running and jumping and climbing they get tired too. God knows that all animals and people need to rest. He wants us to get sleep so we can be healthy and happy. When we sleep, our bodies grow and get stronger. Playing and resting are both important.

What do you say?

• Can you find the sleeping otter in the picture?

• How do otters open the shellfish that they love to eat?

• Where is your favorite place to sleep? What kinds of things do you sleep with?

• Why do you think God wants all of his creation to rest?

What does God say?

I will lie down in peace and sleep, for you alone, O LORD, will keep me safe.
PSALM 4:8

Deep Water Friends

Dolphins are small members of the whale family. Although they swim in the oceans, they breathe air through a special opening in the tops of their heads. They must come to the surface often to take a breath. They usually swim with several other dolphins and leap and dive together in the ocean's waves. Sometimes they even ride the waves like a surfer does! But dolphins also care for one another in a very special way. If one dolphin is hurt, its friends will stay close to it and protect it from harm. They may even push the sick dolphin to the surface, so it can take a breath. If its friends didn't help out, the sick dolphin might drown.

God has given each of us good friends to play with and to help. We all know how wonderful it is to have a good friend when we are feeling lonely, hurt, or sad. God wants us to be good friends to others too. When someone is alone, we can ask him or her to play with us. When someone is sad, we can share a hug or just listen if they want to tell us what is wrong. Good friends are a special gift from God.

What do you say?

• Can you find the place on their heads where the dolphins breathe?

• How has a friend helped you? What could you do to help a friend?

• How do the dolphins help one another?

• Why do you think God wants us to be good friends to one another?

What does God say?

A friend is always loyal, and a brother is born to help in time of need.
PROVERBS 17:17

Singing Whales

Many people think that birds are the best singers in the animal kingdom, but do you know what kind of animal sings the longest and most complicated kinds of songs? It's not a tiny bird, but a thirty-ton humpback whale! These huge sea creatures are longer than a school bus and the songs they sing can be heard underwater for twenty miles! Scientists have listened to whale songs with special microphones and have discovered that a group of male whales located in the same area will often all sing the same song at the same time. The whale songs contain moans, clicks, chirps, creaks, and groans. Sometimes the songs last for ten or fifteen minutes! No one knows exactly why the whales sing. They could be happy or upset or even in love.

Just like the humpback whales, people like to sing too. The Bible tells us that God loves to hear his children sing and make music. Whether our songs are happy or sad, we can enjoy singing them. Making up songs is a great way to share our feelings and even to tell God how much we love him.

What do you say?

• What kind of animal sings the longest songs?

• Why do you think the humpback whales sing?

• What kinds of songs do you like best? Can you sing your favorite song?

• Why do you think God likes to hear his children sing?

What does God say?

I will sing to the LORD because he has been so good to me.
PSALM 13:6

Fishy Neighbors

The cleaner wrasse is a tiny fish with some pretty big friends. Cleaner wrasses live on coral reefs and are sometimes known as "doctor fish" because they are so helpful to their neighbors. Every morning, the cleaner wrasse swims to an open spot on the reef. He does a dance to let the other fish in the area know that he is "open for business." All the larger fish that need to be cleaned that day form a line and patiently wait their turn. One by one, the big fish hold still while the cleaner wrasse cleans the bugs and dead skin off of their bodies. Sometimes, the cleaner wrasse even swims into the mouths of the big fish to clean their teeth!

A cleaner wrasse has to be pretty brave to clean his customers' teeth, especially when his customer is a shark or an eel. But these little fish don't get eaten because sharks and eels know that cleaner wrasses are helpers, not lunch. God wants us to be friendly with our neighbors and to lend them a hand when they need it. Good neighbors come in all shapes, sizes, and colors. It pleases God when we are helpful to all our neighbors.

What do you say?

- Who is being helped by the cleaner wrasses?

- Why are cleaner wrasses sometimes called "doctor fish"?

- Who do you know who could use your help?

- How has God helped you?

What does God say?

For the whole law can be summed up in this one command: "Love your neighbor as yourself."
GALATIANS 5:14

61

Oyster Magic

The oyster is a shellfish that lives in salt water. It doesn't make a sound or move or even look very pretty. But oysters create something that is very valuable. Oysters make beautiful, gleaming pearls. When a tiny grain of sand gets inside the oyster's shell, this grain of sand makes the oyster very uncomfortable. In response to this irritation, the oyster begins coating the grain of sand with something called *nacre*, made of protein and calcium. Layer after layer of nacre coats the grain of sand until, at last, a beautiful pearl is formed. Because of its pain, the oyster creates something precious.

Sometimes things happen in our lives that seem sad or bad like the grain of sand feels to the oyster. Things make us irritated or unhappy. But God says that if we will trust him, he can bring good things out of the bad things that happen to us. He promises to never leave us. We can tell him about the bad or sad things and ask him to help us grow and learn from them. Then we can see God make something beautiful in our lives too.

What do you say?

- Can you find the pearls in the oysters?

- How does an oyster make a pearl?

- What's something sad or bad that has happened to you?

- How do you think God might bring something good from the sad or bad thing in your life?

What does God say?

And we know that God causes everything to work together for the good of those who love God and are called according to his purpose for them.
ROMANS 8:28

63

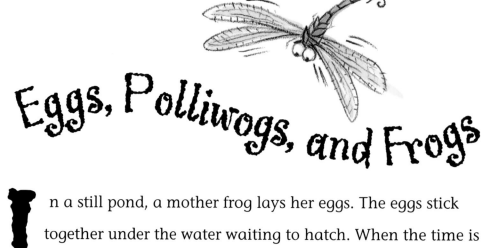

Eggs, Polliwogs, and Frogs

In a still pond, a mother frog lays her eggs. The eggs stick together under the water waiting to hatch. When the time is right, little fish-like animals, called tadpoles or polliwogs, hatch from the frog eggs. They don't look like frogs at all. They have big heads and tails that wave in the water as the tadpole swims in the pond. All day long the tadpole swims and eats and grows. After a while, legs begin to grow on the tadpole. Its body gets longer and its gills begin to disappear. After more time has passed, the tadpole begins to grow front legs and its tail begins to disappear. It looks more like a frog and is called a froglet. Finally, the tail is gone and the frog is all grown up. It breathes air, but it can still swim when it wants to.

God makes all things grow and change. Just like the polliwog, you will get bigger and grow stronger. One day you may even be as tall as your daddy or mommy. Every day you are learning new things. God has wonderful plans for you as you grow up.

What do you say?

• Can you find the frog eggs in the picture?

• What is another name for the tadpole?

• What is something you might like to do when you grow up?

• Why do you think God makes all things grow and change?

What does God say?

So Jesus grew both in height and in wisdom, and he was loved by God and by all who knew him.

LUKE 2:52

65

Hard-Working Turtles

Once a baby sea turtle hatches from its egg, it has to start on a very long journey. Mother sea turtles lay their eggs in the sand at the beach. When the eggs hatch, baby turtles pop out of the sand and inch their way back to the ocean. The trip to the sea is very hard since sea turtles don't have legs or feet—they only have little fins. For a brand new baby turtle marching across the beach on little fins, the smallest pile of sand seems like a giant mountain. And imagine what a crashing wave looks like to a newborn turtle the size of a person's thumb!

Once a new turtle makes it into the ocean, it has to swim for days to find a peaceful patch of kelp where it can rest and grow strong—and that's if it doesn't get eaten along the way. God knows being a baby turtle is hard. If a turtle works hard and doesn't give up, it can grow up to live in a peaceful cove, snacking on seaweed and jellyfish. God knows that being a person can be hard too, but we have to keep working hard and have faith that God wants us to succeed. God will never give up on us, and he doesn't want us to give up either.

What do you say?

- How many sea turtles are running to the sea?

- Why is it hard for a baby turtle to make it to the ocean?

- Have you ever felt like giving up?

- Why does God want us to work our hardest?

What does God say?

We are pressed on every side by troubles, but we are not crushed and broken. We are perplexed, but we don't give up and quit.

2 CORINTHIANS 4:8

67

Animals That Fly Through the Sky

Have you ever wished you could fly? Do you think it would be fun to soar above the treetops? Birds and butterflies are made so they can do just that! God has given each one a special way to get from place to place. When we watch them stretch their wings to flutter or glide on a breeze, we are reminded of God's creative powers. Each animal has just what it needs to travel the way God intended. You do not have wings, but you can walk, skip, hop, or run to get where you need to be. Whenever we move our bodies we can remember to thank God for how wonderfully he has made us.

Monarch Miracle

Have you ever wondered where the beautiful orange and black monarch butterfly comes from? At the very beginning of its life, the butterfly is just a tiny white egg. When the egg hatches, a larva comes out. The larva eats and grows until it is a large, striped caterpillar. The caterpillar attaches itself to a twig and becomes very still. A hard, green covering grows over its body. This is called a pupa, or chrysalis. Inside, the caterpillar is quietly changing. In just a few weeks, the green shell cracks open and a beautiful black and orange butterfly climbs out. It stretches its wings in the sun, and then it flies away.

Who could imagine that a big, striped caterpillar would ever become a graceful butterfly? Just like the caterpillar, we are becoming what God wants us to be. Sometimes it's hard to wait to grow up, but we can trust that God will help us every day. He promises he will always be with us, and he tells us how to live in the Bible. When we believe him and do what he says, he helps us grow and change in all the right ways.

What do you say?

- Can you find the egg, the caterpillar, the chrysalis, and the butterfly?

- What comes out of a chrysalis?

- What do you think you would like to be when you grow up?

- Why is it a good idea to follow God's ways?

What does God say?

"For I know the plans I have for you," says the LORD. "They are plans for good and not disaster, to give you a future and a hope."

JEREMIAH 29:11

71

Helpful Honkers

Geese like to fly in groups across the sky, making their honking sound. When geese travel, they fly together in a *V* formation. There is an interesting reason why they do this. When they fly in a *V*, each goose gets an extra boost from the goose ahead of it. Because of the updrafts created by their flapping wings, the geese can fly much farther together than any one of them could alone. And the honking they do has a purpose too. The geese in the back of the *V* honk to encourage the ones up ahead to keep going. They cheer each other on! When the lead goose gets tired, he will move back and another goose will take his place. By taking turns in the lead, no one goose gets too tired and everyone gets a chance to be the leader.

Geese do many things to help and encourage one another. That's how God made them. People can do many things to help one another too, but sometimes we don't. Some people like to be first all the time. They don't enjoy cheering for others, and they may not even like helping others. These kinds of people could learn a lesson from geese. God is happy when we are kind to one another, helping and encouraging each other.

What do you say?

• How many geese are in the formation in the picture?

• Why do geese fly in a *V* formation?

• Who is someone you could encourage or help?

• Why do you think God might like you to learn a lesson from the geese?

What does God say?

Rejoice. Change your ways. Encourage each other. Live in harmony and peace. Then the God of love and peace will be with you.

2 Corinthians 13:11b

Happy Hummingbirds

Hummingbirds whiz around a garden like bumblebees. They are very tiny—five of them could fit in a person's hand! They have long, thin beaks with sharp tips, and when they fly, their wings move so fast they look like a blur! God planned every part of the hummingbird for a purpose. He made them tiny so they could fit inside flowers. He made their beaks long and thin so they could reach into blossoms and drink their nectar. He gave them speedy, little wings so they could zip from flower to flower. God made hummingbirds that way because he knew what they would need to be happy and healthy.

God knows what we need too. He gave us eyes so we can see beautiful colors and the faces of family. He gave us ears so we can hear music and the voices of our friends. He gave us minds so we can think and wonder and dream, and he gave us mouths so we can speak and sing. God knew just what we would need to be happy, healthy people. That's why he made each part of our bodies according to his wonderful plan.

What do you say?

- What are these hummingbirds doing?

- What do hummingbirds need?

- Can you think of five good ways you can use your hands?

- Why do you think God made you the way he did?

What does God say?

As we know Jesus better, his divine power gives us everything we need for living a godly life.

2 PETER 1:3A

75

Dancing Cranes

For a long time, scientists couldn't figure out what whooping cranes were doing. Every year, during their migration, the tall, skinny birds land and begin hopping up and down, flapping their wings, and twirling around. Sometimes a flock makes a large circle, and all the birds strut and wiggle together in formation. But why, in the middle of a thousand-mile migration, would whooping cranes take time out to act so funny?

It turns out whooping cranes just like to dance! They fly and fly and fly—and that's hard work—but they take time to relax and have fun too. Some people could take a lesson from whooping cranes. They work so hard that they forget to play. God made the whole wide world for us. He wants us to work hard, but he also likes to see us enjoy ourselves. When we take time to play and have fun, we're celebrating what God has given to us.

What do you say?

- How many dancing cranes do you see?

- Why do whooping cranes stop in the middle of their migrations?

- Did you remember to play today?

- Why does God like to see us play?

What does God say?

Always be joyful.
I THESSALONIANS 5:16

A Selfish Bird

Have you ever seen a cuckoo clock? These clocks look like little houses, and near the peak of the roof there is a door. At the hour and half-hour, the door opens and a little toy bird pops out and says, "Cuckoo!" The little bird in the clock is very helpful, but the real bird that the clock is named after is not a very helpful bird at all. The cuckoo is a bird that seems very selfish. When a mother cuckoo wants to lay her egg, she doesn't build her own nest. Instead, she looks for the nest of another bird. Then she lays her egg in that nest and flies away. When the baby cuckoo hatches, it usually shoves all the other eggs out of the nest. Then the cuckoo chick gets all the food and all the attention from its new mother. The cuckoo doesn't care about anyone but itself.

Some children act just like the cuckoo. They take things that aren't theirs, and they want all the attention they can get. When they act this way, others don't enjoy being their friends. God wants us to be happy, and he knows that we are much happier when we share with others and treat them with kindness.

What do you say?

- Can you find the cuckoo?

- What does the cuckoo do to the other birds that live around it?

- What are some things you could do to show that you are not selfish?

- Why do you think God wants his children to share with others and be kind?

What does God say?

Don't forget to do good and to share what you have with those in need, for such sacrifices are very pleasing to God.
HEBREWS 13:16

Trusty Pigeons

Pigeons are no strangers to the city. They fly from the roofs of tall buildings to the benches in parks, looking for bread crumbs and other small bits of food. But some pigeons are highly trained delivery birds. Pigeons can be trained to carry tiny notes in metal bracelets across long distances. They have a very special ability to find their way around without getting lost. People who want to train pigeons to carry messages must first set their pigeons free and hope that the birds will come back.

It takes a lot of trust for a person to set their birds free. After all, it would be very easy for a pigeon to fly away and find a new home. But pigeons are trustworthy. God taught them to always come back to their real home, so a bird trainer can trust his pigeons to return. God wants us to be trustworthy too. Sometimes when we promise to do one thing, we actually feel like doing something else. God wants us to keep our promises; he wants us to be trustworthy. When we keep our promises it makes us more like him, because God is faithful and we can always trust him.

What do you say?

- Which pigeon is carrying a message?

- Why does a bird trainer have to trust his pigeons?

- What is a promise you have made? Are you keeping it?

- Why does God want you to be trustworthy?

What does God say?

Commit everything you do to the LORD. Trust him, and he will help you.
PSALM 37:5

81

Scary Owls

Barn owls are sometimes called the "ghosts of the barnyard." They aren't ghosts at all, but large, white and tan birds that help farmers get rid of pests like rats and mice. The reason people have made up scary stories about barn owls is because when they fly at night, hunting for food, their light feathers seem to glow in the dark. The owls also make spooky sounds like screeches, wails, and hissing. They swoop over fields and meadows just a few feet above the ground and sometimes startle people who might be outside for a walk. Farmers know that owls are their friends and often make special places in their barns where the owls can make their nests.

God knows that when we don't understand things, we often become frightened, especially at night when it is dark. Sometimes we make up scary stories to explain these things. Then we get even more scared! In the Bible, God tells us that he loves us and that we can trust him. He knows that there are many things we don't understand, but he doesn't want us to be afraid. God is with us in the daytime as well as in the night.

What do you say?

• In the picture, can you find the owl that is nesting and the two owls that are hunting?

• Why have people made up scary stories about the barn owl?

• How can trusting God help us when we are afraid?

• What are some things that make you afraid?

What does God say?

But when I am afraid, I put my trust in you.
PSALM 56:3

Animals in the Unseen World

All around us there are little creatures we may not notice. Some of them live in our homes, gardens, or even under the ground. They quietly go about their business, doing what God intended them to do. We may not think they are important because they are not big or loud. But every living thing is important to God and he has a purpose for each of us. It doesn't matter how big or small we are. It is good for us to remember that God's love doesn't depend upon our size or whether other people notice us. No matter who we are, he always sees and loves us.

Disappearing Tails

Geckos are the only lizards that make sounds other than hissing. The noise they make is a clicking that almost sounds like their name: *Geck-o*. Geckos have sticky toe pads that allow them to climb straight up walls and even across ceilings. Geckos have another unusual trait. When a person or animal catches a gecko by the tail, the little lizard drops its tail and runs away. Losing a tail doesn't even hurt the gecko, in fact, it can grow a new one in a few weeks! God has given the gecko a wonderful way to escape from an enemy and keep from getting hurt.

When we are being hurt or are frightened, it is sometimes a good thing to run to a safe place. We cannot leave a part of ourselves behind, but God has given us a way to be safe too. We can tell a grown up that we trust and ask them to help us. We can ask God to help us too. God wants all of his creation to be safe.

What do you say?

• Can you count the geckos in this picture?

• What can the gecko do when he is caught or frightened?

• What is something that frightens you? Where could you go to be safe?

• Why do you think God wants all of his creation to be safe?

What does God say?

The name of the LORD is a strong fortress; the godly run to him and are safe.

PROVERBS 18:10

Little Ladybugs

adybugs like to crawl on leaves and sometimes on people's arms. They are small members of the beetle family, usually less than a quarter of an inch long. They come in lots of colors from red to brown to black, and many of them have small spots on their *elytra*, or wing covers. Ladybugs are a gardener's friend because they eat the small insects that destroy plants. But ladybugs have some strange ways of doing things. They don't have noses, but they smell with their feet! And they do have mouths, but they taste things with their two antennae! The ladybug's way of doing things is different from ours, but she gets along very well.

People like to do things differently too. Not everyone likes the same things or does things in the same way. Sometimes when people do things differently from us, we think they are wrong. We think our way is the right way. But God reminds us that we should enjoy our differences and not criticize others. Sometimes it's fun to try to do things in a new or different way. We might learn something we didn't know before.

What do you say?

- Can you count all the ladybugs in the picture?

- What are some things you do differently from your friends?

- How does a ladybug smell and taste things?

- Why do you think God wants us to enjoy our differences?

What does God say?

Show respect for everyone. Love your Christian brothers and sisters.
1 PETER 2:17A

Unseen Heroes

Many people think that earthworms are yucky and boring. They do not think of these creatures as heroes in the animal kingdom. They only see them wriggle around in the dirt. But these people don't know the whole story. Without worms, the earth would not be able to produce healthy fruits, vegetables, flowers, and trees. All day long, every day, earthworms are like underground farmers. They make holes in the dirt so that air can get into the soil. This is called aerating. They also enrich the soil with their waste products, called castings. Good soil can have as many as one million worms in an acre! Those million worms can eat ten tons of leaves, stems, dead bugs, and dead roots in a year.

Just because we can't see the worms doing their work, doesn't mean they aren't important. Without them, the world would not be as healthy or beautiful. Sometimes people are like that too. Many people do quiet things that are very important. Others may not see what they do; but God sees all the good things, and he knows who the real heroes are. We might worry that we are doing good things but no one seems to notice. God knows what we are doing and will bless us for being unseen heroes.

What do you say?

- Where are all the earthworms in the picture?

- What are some of the good things worms do?

- What are some good things you have done that no one knows about?

- Why do you think God blesses unseen heroes?

tomatoes

What does God say?

Give your gifts in secret, and your Father, who knows all secrets, will reward you.
MATTHEW 6:4

91

Ants, Ants, Ants

Maybe you have seen ants walking on the sidewalk or in the grass—or even in your house. Ants are small, but they are very strong. They can carry something that weighs five times more than they do. Ants spend most of their time working to gather food and taking care of their nest. When a job is too hard for one ant to do, it will go get some other ants to help. Ants don't talk like people, but they can share messages by touching their antennae together and by leaving trails for other ants to smell. When the ants work together, they can carry big things that are too heavy for one ant to carry alone.

Sometimes you may feel small, but you can do work too. You can help at home and at school. When there is a lot of work to do, you might need to ask for help or help someone else just like the ant. It makes God happy when we work together and help each other to do our best.

What do you say?

• What kinds of things are the ants in the picture carrying?

• How much can one ant carry?

• What is a job you can do to help at home or at school?

• Why do you think God wants us to work together?

What does God say?

Take a lesson from the ants, you lazybones. Learn from their ways and be wise!

PROVERBS 6:6

Caught in a Web

The big, black and yellow garden spider finds a place to spin her orb-shaped web. She uses six tiny spinnerets located under her abdomen to produce different kinds of thin spider silk. Some of the strands are used to anchor the web and others are coated with sticky droplets intended to trap unsuspecting insects. When the garden spider has finished building her web, she sits quietly in the center, waiting for a careless insect to fly into her sticky trap. As soon as one does, the spider rushes to it, bites it to paralyze it, and wraps it in a coating of spider silk. She will eat the dead insect later. As soon as she finishes wrapping up her dinner, the spider hurries back to the center of her web to wait for another insect to come along. She has made a perfect trap!

Lies are a lot like spider webs. They trap the people who tell them. When we tell lies, we feel caught just like the careless insect in the spider's web. But we don't have to worry about being caught in a lie. We can choose to be truthful instead. Telling the truth is the best way to stay out of the web of lies.

94

What do you say?

• What happens when an insect is caught in a spider's web?

• What is caught in the garden spider's web?

• What happens when we tell lies?

• Why do you think God wants his children to tell the truth?

What does God say?

Then watch your tongue! Keep your lips from telling lies!
PSALM 34:13

95

Animal Index